Praise for *Exile Home, That Tra* *Map of the Winds,* and **Mark Sta**

It's very rare to watch the birth of a new style. It's like watching through new set of Proust's kaleidoscopes. Mark Statman has been working for years on a vision of himself and parts of the city—concentrated and bare as any poetry. It's hard to compare it to anything else.

—David Shapiro

Sieve-like and shifty language with more directness and clarity than obfuscation and obtuseness. The father poem of *Exile Home,* "Green Side Up," is a triumph of courage and poetry and love. From it the manuscript opens like a flower of multiple petals. I am enthralled by a seeming innocence and a creeping wisdom, which, rather than distort the innocence, strengthens it. After all, we have the choice to see the world as unconcerned about our troubles in it. It is the world, not a bark on which we float toward happiness. An assertion of the will to see hope as language-driven, music-clad. Mr. Yeats and his wind-up birds. There are many drowsy emperors out there.

—Pablo Medina

To date, in spite of an incredibly productive and much lauded career as a poet, Mark Statman's greatest claim to fame is his astonishing translation, with Pablo Medina, of García Lorca's *Poet in New York. Exile Home* changes all that."

—John Yamrus

Although the poems in Mark Statman's lovely *That Train Again* break down into sections and titles, you could almost read this book as a long, sweet poetic day of meditation; earth sky, birds, winds, wife, love, and the ways they attach themselves to the poet and, through him, to us. A good book of poetry will urge us not to miss the fine details. Here is music to slow the pulse and re-tune the ear to what is important.

—Cornelius Eady

Mark Statman's spare, candid poems speak of the ways a person moves "from fold/into blue." *That Train Again* details out daily translation of "world/into world."

—Idra Novey

Mark Statman's voice brings together historical awareness with mindful surrender for the present moments (that sometimes calls back memories from psyche's depths). Mark Statman's lines are maps of the wind that carry us into wonder and love.

—Aliki Barnstone

Sung through a register of gentle if unrelenting consciousness on the part of the poet that the present is always inexhaustibly on the move, Statman's spare, concise, searching poems channel notations of experience through the visual and aural senses.

—Anselm Berrigan

Statman's voice is a kind of spare lyricism that reminds me of the ancient Greek poets of the Anthology or the concise voicings of Antonio Machado.

—Joseph Stroud

...an admirably light touch illuminates the seriousness behind the poems...

—Tony Towle

Mark Statman delivers the tourist's wonder and distance in spare deliberate music—American's grand plain poetry descended from William Carlos Williams to James Schuyler. Statman is a head-on poet willing to risk clarity in pursuit of the marvelous we might encounter anywhere.

—William Corbett

Statman gives us language as commitment, commitment as imagination, imagination as soul-making.

—Joseph Lease

Mark Statman's new book *Exile Home* is a love poem, a snapshot, to the poet's adopted country so fresh in the poem "Mi México". The air, the light, the poignancy of little girl with wooden bowl, & mystery of life next to another, a beloved partner, buzz with sharp grace. A contrast across the border, with family loss, but no walls, here. Power of "all the unseen... writ in glass in water clouds" join the fiesta. No ideas but in things. I want to go there too. This is a sweet and pungent sensory exile, almost a dream.

—Anne Waldman

Exile Home is an elegiac journey of discovery: "the room/ that lights/ the house" is the possibility of coming to be who you are in whatever place we find ourrselves. These are poems of transition as a form of mediation and meditation. Mark Statman's short lines mark the flux of sentiment as openness to what's next. "can you believe/ we live like this?" Only time tells.

—Charles Bernstein

Mark Statman's fiercely elegiac book begins with the long poem, "Green Side Up," dedicated to his father. Written in lower case with no punctuation, it provides quick flashes of family memory and the present reality of grief. The reader is utterly absorbed and lifted: "on the phone/ you say it's/ another DIP/ day in paradise/ waking early enough/ there were no/ sounds of morning/ only birdsong breeze/ the meaning of paradise/ that first moment/ alone and taking in/ coffee and sunlight." This is realism in the most beautiful sense. We are taken to the living moment as it passes. Italo Calvino wrote of "the moral values invested in the most tenuous traces." It's in "the intensity of minor acts" (John Ashbery) that we are folded into the cloak of truth: "we did this/ we did this/ it happened/ before we thought it." It was "a voice made for radio": "Al Statman here/ good morning."

—Paul Hoover

At his best, Mark Statman whimsically seduces us to plug what large emptiness we carry into the day. Such a playfulness of spirit and sound, not yet outlawed in these parts, lifts us toward some unforeseen feeling or study of human life that would have eluded us, were it not for his sparse and controlled lines. Here is an eclectic imagination that redeems the conventional exploits of language and all the dead zones around us. *Exile Home* consecrates Statman's forever voice.

—Major Jackson

Exile Home

Poems

Mark Statman

Lavender Ink
New Orleans

Exile Home
Mark Statman

Copyright © 2019 by the author and Diálogos Books.

All rights reserved. No part of this work may be reproduced in any form without the express written permission of the copyright holders and Diálogos Books.

Printed in the U.S.A.
First Printing
10 9 8 7 6 5 4 3 2 1   19 20 21 22 23 24

Book design by Bill Lavender.
Cover Art: by Katherine Koch

Library of Congress Control Number: 2019935039
Statman, Mark
Exile Home / Mark Statman;
p. cm.
ISBN: 978-1-944884-61-1 (pbk.)

Lavender Ink
lavenderink.org

Acknowledgements/notes

My decision to move to Mexico in September 2016 was both personal and professional. In May 2016, at the age of 54, my friend, the poet and scholar, Robin Mookerjee, died, suddenly, unexpectedly. We had taught together for some two decades in the Literary Studies department at Eugene Lang College at The New School in NYC. At that point, I'd just finished my 31st year teaching at the College.

It was Robin's death that set everything in motion. I'd already started to think that sometime soon it might be time to make some changes, but Robin dying, and just 54, really got me started. I was just a few weeks shy of my 58th birthday. After 31 years at Lang, suddenly, very suddenly, I realized the seriousness of that question, what comes next? I knew that one day my life would no longer include teaching. And that led me to thinking, Hillel-like, if not now, why not? If not now, when? I had no good answers for not making the changes. With (relative) youth on our side, my wife, the painter and writer, Katherine Koch and I decided to sell our Brooklyn home of 25 years. We would move to Oaxaca, a small city in the south of Mexico, capital of the state of the same name which we have been visiting since 1986. We would become permanent residents there. Our son, the musician, Jesse "Cannonball" Statman, would accompany us, help set up our new home, before taking off on a 4 month tour of the US and Europe. We'd be bringing with us our two Labrador retrievers. Sadly, in March 2017, the older one, the zen-like Cannonball, from whom our son took his stage name, died just before his 14th birthday. We were glad his last year was spent away from the NYC winter, spent warm, comfortable, sleepy days on a sunny patio.

There were ins and outs to the process, the fears, the

strangeness of becoming an expatriate, of no longer living in one's own country, of leaving NYC, where Katherine and I had each lived most of our lives. But we did have a number of things going for us. One of them we knew Oaxaca, and we liked what the city is and has become—a good literary scene, a good arts scene, a good music scene. There is good food. It's a beautiful city, small (400,000) but culturally very cool. It has a history of indigenous independence, of occasional radical politics (which is off-limits to us, as permanent residents, we can't get involved in Mexican politics though the U.S. is more than fair game and we do our best to make our voices known—as citizens, we still vote in all elections in Brooklyn, since that is our last U.S. residence). We know people down here, Mexican and US poets, painters, etc. There is even a Lang graduate here (2003), a very well-known musician (internationally) who is one of our closest friends—she was Jesse's baby sitter when he was 4, she was a student of mine for two semesters, and, in the fun stories department, she has a wonderful child, now older than Jesse was when she baby sat for him, who seems to take a certain delight in hanging out with us.

I also knew that I wasn't precisely retiring, just that I was not going to teach anymore and I would devote myself to writing and translating. So I'd have work to do. When we moved down that September, I had three books left on my current book contract, one now with this current poetry collection, so the change from our old life didn't mean wholesale break. We can afford to live here. We rent a big house in Oaxaca Centro (4 bedrooms, courtyards, patio, tons of storage) and we bought a small house in the country with some land that is quite beautiful, very rural, we're surrounded by farms and fields, with goats, sheep, oxen, horses grazing, but only a 25-30 minute drive to the big house in the city center.

I write, a lot, more than I have in many, many years. I read, and the reading is deeper than it's been for a while because I no longer think about teaching; the question, how would I teach this poem, this idea, no longer (or hardly ever) comes up. It's reading that matters in my own small and large schemes. Katherine paints, gardens, writes. She reads as well, again, a lot. We are those people who divide their lives between the country and the city. We see friends, go to parties. We go on day trips to ruins, churches, little towns. We go to the beach on occasion (about 120 miles away but a six hour drive because we are in the mountains, a mile high, and you go through a bunch of ecosystems, rainforest etc. to get to the Pacific). We've driven to the US a few times, a nice long drive that takes one through the middle of Mexico, mountains, deserts, volcanoes. There seem to be lots of folks visiting here. We've had friends from the US because of Oaxaca's deserved rep as a cultural center.

It goes without saying that a defining moment of this book was the sudden, surprising death of my father, Albert Statman, who died in March 2018. I had thought so often of hikes he and I would take, of the food we'd eat, of the pleasure he would have taken in visiting us. "Green Side Up" is the poem that starts this book, that frames it.

This book is a reflection on those changes. I think of Exile and Home as verbs and nouns. We came here out of desire, out of a sense of the next adventure. But I miss Brooklyn, and yet the Brooklyn I miss no longer exists. It is strange and extraordinary to live someplace where every day is a cultural and linguistic delight.

So many people to acknowledge: first my fiery band of readers: Pablo Medina, Joseph Lease, Katherine Koch, John Yamrus, and Marshall Malin. Their advice and critiques helped me understand what is here. I also want to thank the wonderful

Oaxaca poet Efraín Velasco Sosa for his friendship and our regular Friday coffee/tea at Café Brujula where we talk about poetry, art, politics, family, life. Reto Bissegger gives us the Manta Raya and the beautiful hidden beach at Salchi where I did a good deal of the revising of this Exile Home. *Un abrazo grande y besos besos besos* to Isahrai Azaria and Elby who have extended our family here and made our lives so much richer. Many thanks as well to Arya Francesca Jenkins—part of these notes come from an interview we did last year for her blog writersnreaders. I am grateful, as well to Ralph Adamo for publishing the full text of "Green Side Up" in the *Xavier Review*. Paul Hoover generously published a number of these poems in *New American Writing*. Some of these poems also appeared in *Live Mag* and I thank Jeff Wright for that. I know I am missing some others—I will correct these for future editions.

Sometimes the old life keeps going. In the spring of 2017, the Board of Trustees at the New School generously appointed me the first ever Emeritus Professor at Eugene Lang College where I had taught for so long. An honor. The great awards life offers.

The words I have for Katherine are, of course, throughout this book, and that's why this book is for her. It is also for Jesse, our son, who, as a musician, lives so much life on the road; he remains a surprise and joy. His support of his father the poet means a lot.

This is my 5th book with Bill Lavender, extraordinary editor, poet, friend. His faith in my poetry is a great gift.

Also by Mark Statman

The Red Skyline (poems)

Listener in the Snow: The Practice and Teaching of Poetry

The Alphabet of the Trees: A Guide to Nature Writing (co-edited with Christian McEwen)

Poet in New York, Federico García Lorca (translated with Pablo Medina)

Tourist at a Miracle (poems)

Black Tulips: The Selected Poems of José María Hinojosa (translation)

A Map of the Winds (poems)

That Train Again (poems)

Never Made in America: Selected Poems from Martín Barea Mattos (translation)

Exile Home

for Katherine

Green Side Up

for my father, Al Statman (1933-2018)

1.

that was the joke
the saying
to look out the
window to think the
green side is up
there's the sun
there are the mountains
dry and bright in
your Arizona

2.

take with you
your stickball
memories Brooklyn
Bronx you
wake up from a
hospital dream you'd
hit two sewers something
won

3.

on the phone
you'd say it's
another DIP
day in paradise
waking early enough

there were no
sounds of morning
only birdsong breeze
the meaning of paradise
that first moment
alone and taking in
coffee and sunlight

4.

growing up I
would sit with you
at the kitchen table
pre-dawn you ate
cereal it was
before you were
off to work I
thought I should
sit with you someone
should sit with
you I would
then you'd go off
to work I'd go
for a run or
back to sleep who
remembers what we
said I remember
silence

5.

a kiss and a
bop on the head
it's what you gave us

then that last kiss
no bop you
were already too
weak you couldn't
move your hands
but you could kiss
you could smile that
smile that split your
face the world
in two

6.

what did you
say that for
breakfast your
father had a
shot of whiskey
an onion then
off to the bakery
ready for the
work of the
day

7.

water one of
your elements
watching you from
the shore as you
dove into one wave
after another like
some water god

8.

but one day we
were swimming
across a boat channel
in the Florida Keys
you said
I'm in trouble
who was always there
to save us from trouble
I hailed a passing
boat they pulled us in
your first heart
attack your first
trouble the many
troubles the gods fall
gods always fall they
are meant to fall they
are meant to give us
stories and disappear

9.

and Mom is crying is
angry is grief she
wanted to be
the first to go she
wanted you to be
the one to live alone
that isn't how she
means it but the
loneliness you've left her
you hid your cancer

you did this
to everyone

never wanting to be
thought as sick
never wanting to be
the problem

10.

when you turned forty
you joked
well now I guess
I'll never play centerfield
beloved DiMaggio
beloved Mantle
beloved Yankees

11.

my sons my
legacy my
history you
said to the doctor
have you met
my son the poet?

there dying you
let me know you
knew

12.

singing lines from

musicals movies Broadway
the night they invented champagne

13.

your voice was
made for radio
or we imagined
so I imagine
I can hear it now
going out across
the airwaves
Al Statman here
good morning

14.

nothing ahead and
nothing behind
which is to say
present which is
to say nothing at
all except this
holding your hand
holding you hold
onto life a
little longer

15.

you opened your eyes
you were in so
much pain you said
did you ever think
your father was

such a baby?

16.

it didn't matter
the story you just
loved to tell
a story
or maybe it
was all the stories
maybe you were saying
here is
your inheritance

17.

driving through
Canada on the way
to Montreal you
bought a beret and
sang *Frere Jacques*
one time ten times
a hundred times
a secret happiness that
wasn't secret

18.

I'd call your phone
you'd say hello and
ask me how I was doing
then you'd say
here's your mother and
I'd say but dad
I'm calling you

19.

who goes rock hunting?
we go rock hunting
driving along
Long Island back roads
looking for boulders
we'd heave into the car
to decorate the yard

20.

when you were a boy
davening in *shul*
an old man behind you
smacked your head
because in your
broken Hebrew, he said,
you'd called God a
son of a bitch

21.

I don't want to
forget anything
not your anger
not your love
I don't want
to forget
maybe I disappointed you
Sunday mornings growing up
you made pancakes
we listened to
NY football Giants games
names like

Ron Johnson
Fran Tarkenton
Spider Lockhart

22.

we asked you
what you did at work
you said
I sharpen pencils

23.

you talked about your
golf game but
I never saw you play
you were proud of
the athlete me
once I overheard
you say to a friend
have you ever seen Mark run?

24.

when you decided
you'd had enough
you said you
wanted to go home
to leave the hospital
no more tubes no more
machines no more
beeping sounds
you were going to die
in the sounds of
your own house

the familiar the loved
you had the voices there
of your family who
had come to say
we love we love we love
who had come to say
please and stay and
then goodbye

25.

you told me
the story of
Becky under the stairs
the first girl ever kissed

26.

in the hospital
I shaved you
you hadn't shaved
in days gray
stubble gray
skin and you
looked somehow
better almost ready
to live
I cleaned your glasses
filthy when you came home
I fed you strawberries
blueberries later
David did the same
the last food you'd
eat on earth

27.

what worried you
you wouldn't say
except finally in
your final days
take care of your mother
take care of your mother
it had been your job
more than sixty-five years
and now could you
trust your sons?
but how could we
the way you could?
how could we manage
her suddenly empty life?

28.

you loved having been
Air Force you
never talked about it
but when all your sons
were small you would
lift us up
lift us high you'd
sing: *into the air*
junior bird man
into the air
upside down

29.

to see
your coffin

to touch
your coffin
to spill earth
on your coffin
to see the
row after row
of graves to
see the rolling green of
this military cemetery
to know your
green side
is above to know
I think each day
green side up
I mean
I think of you

Exile Home

I. El adiós de siempre (Brooklyn)

breaking in

last night
it's dreaming
Brooklyn our
old house
of things left
behind
we needed
to throw away
needed
to destroy
of ourselves
of 5th Street of home
no longer home
what there is
who
there is no

what comes
is
crossing out
we cross out
the old home
to make
the new
cross

the old
to see still
what was
there
we cross
the old
go forward

for the celebration

we've fallen
down the mountains
of grace
become divers
of fame underwater

we can't seek
in twilight
destiny or stars
we gave away
at the end of holy days
what we
left on the
tables of
our homes

the ride back
the radio played
news music
at a break
the announcer said

turn off the sound
at the fork in
the road where it's
sky where it's
sky where

narrative

no need to get
too caught in
questions of
sequence
because the stories
always land somewhere else:
a forest in Brazil
an island in Vermont
a doozy of a night
on a calm ocean
a coast elsewhere
with barely breaking waves
we drank a lot we talked
a bank failure a heart failure
failures of spirit
failures of soul you asked me
where are all the good men
and when you said
I'd better to get to
know you then
I don't think I replied

what will make a difference

because different maybe
how you say there's a word in French
I repeat it but in Spanish
then in English I remember
I thought how in front of us
we'd had not the image of the moon
but the moon itself
and then not the image of the sun
but the sun rising
I thought look at the sun
with the whole late night sky
in its light

suave patria

for Efraín Velasco Sosa

no man is an island
no woman
no child

is river is cloud
is mountain is ocean

uncontained unwept
untouched all are

by sound
and cruelty
by love and poetry

the kind of love
held in one's arms

the kind of cruelty
that comes with
the territory of hope
with threat desire

the poem
makes proposals
for the world:
take hold watch

when ice breaks in spring
what if
there is no spring

no renewal no rain
what where there is
no ice
a blessing

was the morning
moon the
midday sun the
march of over and
blood far away we
don't have to hear
and smell it what
we know we know
by word of mouth

from ear to ear
we learn
the cold has come and
the snows have come
the trees have broken
from the weight from
ice we have longed
to be far away
and now like that
the days

carry fire

consciousness is a wound
or a wound
is wind
a wound within the wind

everything we know
has to leave
some sadness
behind
the sadness of
either pain
either longing

so we cry and
morning bird-like hope
for sun and rain
for sun and rain
to carry

I focus and

rein in memories of
my self different
times different places
but how is it
I see my face how is it
memory showing
impossible visions

I should
see a dirt road I
should see
mountain views a
beach see from the top of
skyscrapers from buildings
rising from sidewalk Brooklyn
I should see a
body your body not mine

I should not see me
not as child or man
not as in mirror
this is wrong
this remember

well

now that the beach still is
full of mystery and
that boy over there

has gone completely silent
the silence makes
waves against the waves of
ocean water

here will be a
closing and craziness
splendor of
night
of stars and
moon of
something phosphorescent
rising from
the water like
something out of that dream
the one from which you
wake startled with
the whole world suddenly
in tune

you were funny she said

as if you
weren't anymore but
you realized
that wasn't what
she meant
she was
talking about
the past
not anything

in the present
and you wondered
a little more
about all the times
you hadn't
understood the
situation and you'd
wondered then what
in life
remained lost and missing

territory

a blonde day of
no account
as we stumble
the rocks
spheres sapphires
unlocked accents
no one can place
no one knows
who you are
you could
be anyone
celebration and odyssey
that build into
days in which
life says
rest
from your
omega alpha gamma

I can't wake up

from this sleep
debilitating dream
faces in masks no voices
dream silence opens
my heart closes
my heart a weakening
body how to take a
breath who is to
take a breath to
come up for air how
do you do that in
a world that is
no world how to stop
stop stop this can't be
real this unreal this real
the repeating faces
coming to me a
choking sleep in
bitterness where there's
crying where's the tears

other debts

I was thinking
of an old friend today
how I owe him a call
I owe him a dinner a drink
I still have some of his books

then I realized
he was dead
and I realized even more
the need to find a way
to pay him back

pay him
pay everyone
because one day
I won't be able
to pay anyone anymore

I walked a long time today
I walked hills and
the city

I thought of nothing
I needed to do so much
to do something and all
there was was nothing

then

we stood on a bridge
over the Seine
where lovers would
leave their keys
their locks
or keys and locks

but we had

neither
needing neither
we had
the bridge and sky
each other
we had
November morning
the Seine

to philosophy

the trick
to know the names of
the cities and the poets
to say
in the coming year
the names of
ghosts the
names of
our dead
to tell them no
they are not lost or
forgotten we have
made a shelter of
trees and stones
here for them
to rest

two years ago

I was sick

later my doctor said
it really had been
life and death
that I could
have gone what
would that have
meant

one day I'll
know I'll know
we'll all
know but
every day that
day needs to be
a little farther
down the line

I realized

I'm not afraid
of death but
loss—what if there's
none of this this
music of the world—
morning sounds morning
sun morning slowness
and day
what if one is all
alone no love no
poetry

into the sand

water drips
ghostly
presence we may be
unequal to the task
of the day

we founder
on shores
whose names
we don't know
we imagine we
drift toward
new worlds
not knowing
if our boats
have names
we unthinking
guide them
we go forward
desire to replace
or add to what we
already carry

maybe you looked

out the window
from the bus
you waved at
me but I

didn't see maybe the
gray windows or I
wasn't looking I
was moving on
to whatever
was next
I didn't know
once how
all we have in
life we never
lose we
gather we collect
we keep I
do that now
now I know
it's all still there
real and living

in the beginning

I am not
wilder than love
nor than kisses

not wilder than wine
nor wild days
nor wilder than the trees
nor the storms in the trees
the broken branches
the broken roots
the falling leaves

the falling flowers

I'm not wilder than
cars and trucks
trucks and trains
a city beach
the street's traffic
the city river

wild people everywhere
they jump the earth
off the earth
language and dance
they spring

why this axis?
why this spin?
waters rising
waters rise
we run to the edge
of our own
landmarks our own
frontiers
before we cross
the border think:
are we wild
are we ready

to be in the wild
the wild
to be at the start of history

the start of undone creation?

etc.

the longest days
seem not to have
useful meaning
you can throw them
all away but who
pays attention
right now
maybe I should say
I don't feel well
that will let something
else happen
but the days and days
go and
no one can stop that
words come and go
water does too air
time comes goes science
art the ways of
explaining simple things
the weather death maps
I thought maybe
getting out of bed
would help me figure
out all the simplicity
of simple action
but the rattling windows
in the wind say

a different game a
wedding of dream and fire
sleep and voice
I wonder about
the clue the secret
I've been wondering and
would like to be
told it's been here in
a box next to morning

a growing wish

words
from the past
take hold in
mysterious ways
today *hinausgegangen*
and to have left
to be out and on
my way be on the
road on the fly
it happens
we travel we trail
we travail
we set up bookkeeping
in small fortress corners
small our own
universe we
account for what
will go   and go
go on

we remember to think
of these
days to remember

Einstein dream

he wasn't surprised
by anything
it was his thing
long after
most of us
had gone to bed

what would he change here?

the curtains maybe
the arrangement of
chairs

he held out
his hand
a gesture
and presented his
hypothesis

that everything
would be all right
he said this
not as a scientist
but as spirit soul man
as someone

on the move
who knew

beauty may not

be enough
the things
of this world
up against
everything we
do reminds us how
who we are
is by our doing how
looking for *is*
who we
are how looking
for what's
left is
how we
so become

poetry in pursuit of justice

rides horseback
rides bareback
rides bare
rides erotic rides exotic
rides
through the fields around
rides the train
rides the bus

rides in back of a truck
too many people
on their way
to somewhere
and we never know where
or the truck disappears or
the people disappear we
only later know their
names but who
will recognize who
will forgive

it was in the news last night
though it's been there
all the time
it's one story
a repeating story
they're all repeating stories
human consequential
still unknown
like the unknown poets
the unknown citizens
the unknown souls
we're all
from other places
and other times
which makes
the big picture the hard picture
impossible and maybe not
even worth pursuing
but if the

small picture is too small
if the big picture
keeps invading imploding
what to do
with all that
without creating
the certainty of failure
or another kind of solution
for what works or
what matters or
what will change the
very course of time

who longs for time
who longs for history
who longs for consequences
with wars and peace
with all the leftover
voices whose voices
go fading fading into
a different consciousness
a different longing

we could sell
longing for longing
we could sell
body for body
we could dwell and predict
or live somewhere else
some place where
everything is somehow far away

maybe that's another ride
another life
without all
the temptation
of hope
the willingness
to wonder
in which world
we'll end

which is how
it always ends
with endings
it's what
happens before
we can call poetry
or pursuit
or justice
which are
their own ends greater
always always

someone

you know
unexpectedly
dies

you
get

the news you
gasp just
stop
but and
oh for

someone suddenly
memory
no body no
tomorrow

casting sin

the river
was full
of stones
we walked
over
if it
was full of
fish I
wouldn't know
my line forever
snagging weeds
I care
I should care
but not
enough that
way not enough
that morning

you want to know

how to avoid
today's sadness
without running to
retreat you want
to know how to
avoid the day
to think
the future isn't
so hard
to run around and
look the never-
falling sky

when I think of all the years

a squadron of sunlight
and on the other side
of the sky the moon
we could get there
in our boat
but we wouldn't know then
what to do
no bread no meat no wine
like the movement of a clock
clockwork
the idea of good manners enters
a contest a struggle
with good breeding
Apolito is a mighty breed

a chocolate Lab
I'm one of the Cohanim
not a breed or a tribe
but a class a caste
a priest
without a temple to
make sacred

where should we go?

there is no perfect sky
no perfect clouds
no perfect dreams
no perfect roof
no perfect clause
or antidote
there may be no
antidotes at all
the ones we know
used are useless
a waste of time
deserving no
time in the world
though that depends
on all the world
the constellations
the change fortune solitude
the constellations
with heroes and their
heroic lives their
recorded galaxy histories

which despite the
records despite the
stars we forget we forget

I want with
my hands/a price
a sculpture/a blade
a boulder/a carcass
a rock/a bottle
anything with destination

nothing is almost:
tragedy goal hope destiny
which means how easy
after wandering into
trouble to
wander away

night fall

what goes with you when
you go what do you
leave behind what do
you hold onto what

pots pans knives winter
clothes bookcases books what
tables chairs a couch a bed what
given forgiven we

sat on the stoop and neighbors

and friends of decades they
refused to believe *how*
can you leave this

your Brooklyn skyline your
Brooklyn sky your

el adiós de siempre

the pins were dropping everywhere
as if
there was no future
to speak of anymore
that this was a circle
or a cube
or a glass jar
in which we'd put
some fireflies
or some sparks of stone
or a god
once worshipped

moved by the earth
and of it
our sadness
grows
lengthening
not so much like a dream
but a trial
by cold and wind
an enormous burden

someone has to carry
as a perfect fact
of what shouldn't
happen in life

last century I
almost wanted to give up
thought maybe all my life
was coming apart

except it didn't
and now it won't
I can say that because
that's what's left
to believe
my belief is fear-proof
my fears can't touch
our future

II. The middle of a different story (Oaxaca)

fair to say

living in
two languages
creates
a third
like living
in two houses

or like
the way
I am
in love
with the
presence
of love
so here
so many
years
is a
singular love
though
like the sky
like the earth
unchanging
and unchanging
with all

the lived-in rooms
and all
the words

the twist of fate

the air is
full with
ribbons the
colors of
Mexico and
not the USA and
I don't mind
I'm
in the middle of
a different story
one where
the ribbons come
down the
stars come down the
story full of
blessings we are
the blessed
this air full of
songs of
red white green
in ribbons

of the sounds outside

I think

flowers flowering
the trees
with orange
always orange and
white purple red
it's a willingness
the flowers have
to show themselves off
as we walk by or
we just sit
we say
listen
those trees
those flowers

lyric

think of
what it
was like
for us
before each
day started
buen día
another life
another world
now what
we say
good morning
good day
buen día

night manners

with all the
barking dogs
on their
barking rooftops
you wonder
how the owners
survive
the noise
the piercing
the constant
loyal menace

I chose

to put
some words
over here the
way we
decided to
move the plants in
macetas around
the patio some
need sun and
others shade
we want
it all just right

one star at a time

all I can

do with
the sky is
stare or
watch or wonder
or give
myself over
to the feeling
that it's all
too big or all
too much to
understand the

way
life is like
that each moment
at a pace
and I think
did a year just
pass
or was it a
minute
there are

dances
and poses
there's Ares and
Jupiter
there's Roberto
Juan and Jorge

who aren't stars

they're just
here to paint
the house
Juan arrived a
little after eight
he stood outside waiting
he'd rung the
bell he'd knocked
but upstairs we hadn't
heard not
expecting anyone
so early

money doesn't grow on trees

the primeval is restricted
by the primary
or is it the reverse?
the colors of tomorrow
hint at a world
overrun with lakes a symphony
it's how we get better
from this or that illness
as bric-a-brac and
promise
the name tag says
hello, do you know who I am?
not a notebook full of words
not a whole new solar system
on the solar system map
not the sky or the universe

maybe the infinity lost as I look at
cloud after cloud

strangers

fill the streets because here
for the day of the dead
the tourists want
spectacle want parades
and music they want
to wear the
orange *muertos* flowers
that are everywhere
there are altars covered with orange
and covered with photos food old
clothes jewelry dishes
the tourists come they spend
their money then
they go away and the
streets a little
empty

nothing useless

a man on the street
whistles the birds whistle
the train whistles
the kettle
and that broom there
sweeps the day
away

sweeps the dust
the street
the street
full of noise
full of the man
full of his whistle
which is
a passion song
a passion play
not *the* passion play
but a play some
of us know
a song of a lark
a call of a jay
the cry of
a whole day
in its morning
that cries lover
come back to me
and cried so
suddenly
all the lovers do
and
suddenly sadly
the world is in love
we are all in love
and loving
whistling down the
street
incredible
we did this

we did this
it happened
before we thought it

spontaneously

morning
and the rows of life
are not in exile
or flame or ice
but on these streets
not empty anymore
not silent anymore
but contemplative slow
because it's not a circus yet
still early enough
so the man selling ices
is still not quite in place
still a little by himself
the sun hasn't
even yet burned the
clouds away

it didn't rain here
two night ago
but my doctor she said
it had in Cuilapam
then it rained here last night
and now the streets so clean
they are ready for the
morning parade the

daily ebb and flow of walkers
and vendors on Llano park
marching bands
shoeshines
palm trees and bursting fountains
children at play
dogs at play
sky at play
in the everyday play

did it rain in her town
last night the way it had here
did it rain on her streets of
Cuilapam de Guerrero
are hers full now of fiesta
full clean and bright like here
when next
we meet I'll have to ask
la doctora

translation (an introduction)

you
fall

in love

in love

the hard bop

every song
goes somewhere
every song amen
a point denying doubt
in a world so
full and music
images

of density of sorrow
of someone else's eternal
return and who
wouldn't want to return
or at least travel
to someplace one has already been
a revisit where
what was a surprise or
happiness can calm
the sick heal the
sick we can take the
sickness we can travel
the world we can make
the world well
whoever knows something about this
should come forward not
out of the rain
—it hasn't been raining—
but out of the night
maybe into a sun whose
light is everywhere now it's

an amazing thing to watch
how this day comes to us

when is

the time
to hold
you to turn
down the
music turn
the lights
we do
this we
always do
this
so many nights
hours
years we
have held
each other we

words in order to live

what we have
really what I have
in my head
or on this page
is a story
some story
any story
to be told

when we're all
sitting around
hoping that
we matter
more than the
dangers of
our imaginations
our shoulders
to the wheel
of the place
where we
have all
put down
the roots
we've held up
in the air
put down
in the earth
breathe a little
the silence of
the days still in
the days

this could

be one of those
days I begin
to decide
to remember my age
to walk as
long but slower

to say hey
body remember
all those good
times
remember
we've had them
they've had us
we don't need
to do that
stuff again

thinking

no mistakes this time

as prelude

to the next

big one

like when I start

to concentrate

I know

my mind

will drift

will drift

there goes

a car

into

the wrong lane

taken by surprise?

taken

to one of those mornings

pasear pasear pasear

memory before me

who wants

to go for a walk/*pasear*?

Apollo who leaps up/in/to/from

his days of doze and play

wear and tear

the body accumulates facts

like weather and
the names of trees
of flowers of birds
or walks taken and
food eaten
it accumulates the smells of the world
of garbage
a flowing river
of soap of cologne

accumulates the
voice of the lover the
voice of the bus driver
the truck driver the
voices of kids and
their morning walks to school

sometimes it's happiness
and sometimes it isn't
like seasons changing
which here in southern Mexico
the changes are not the same as memories
of summer heat to fall chill
of fall chill to winter cold and
then there's the first snow

why always such a surprise
as kids we used to
run to the windows and
the teachers would say
hey it's just snow

but they wouldn't stop us
not the good teachers at least
because they were happy too
to see the snow accumulate

the Mexico sky is so
beautiful clear and blue
the mountain morning chill
will warm soon into day
that sun you have
to see it brilliant
in the sky and
we walk through
the day as the day
moves on

try

make the most of
this quiet
not every
night will be like
this not every night
this peace

telescoping

everything
to some
vision
the tumbling down

the hill
the
tumbling of cities
of dew
in the morning
on grass
over grass
on leaves
over leaves

today in dry and
lovely heat
could be
cruel or gentle
maybe I'll know the
difference
after the morning
after the sun

maybe how
we enter greatness is
to be more of
the day
to resist
whatever isn't it

so this was last night's question

it's wonderful
falling
asleep

on the couch
waking
suddenly
with a smile
how thinking
after that
first
confusion
yes
here
here
here I
am

now I'm tempted

we'll wrap the
ends of night
into some brute
style some great
emptiness a well
or an earthquake and
the music will
change to
an apostrophe
longer than life
someone will
find and discover
and scream
and the world
should know

waking depressed

is unexpected
these Mexico days
that one after
another continue
in beauty
so waking now
unpleasant surprise

cohetes

fiesta season
from July to
January
celebrating
revolution
or independence
celebrating
taxi drivers
postal workers
communions
virgins

for six seven
months
daily
music processions parades
no matter
the time
sunrise noon

sunset midnight
it's always
someone's
cocktail hour
someone's fiesta
someone's parade
always
music
always
the band
always these
rockets
exploding

trying to write about time passing

how to do it
where everything seems to
remain the same

even in rainy season sun
yes the dry season has no
clouds it's that I still
don't recognize the signs
time marked by the
next fiesta by saints by food
by the next parade
by history

not spring green not
summer light not

fall orange yellow not
winter freeze and ice

yesterday and yesterday and
yesterday and
tomorrow tomorrow tomorrow
always present

like this passing years

this is not us

in exile but
choice though I
think for a
while it did seem
we were forced we
were ripped
from Brooklyn
our Brooklyn my
with
night walks of
brownstones and
lights of familiar the
trees and sky

I will always be
from Brooklyn I will
never be Oaxaqueño
but here I am
I think for

the rest of my
life
it has been
a lovely Christmas season
 with its lights
 and music
 (its oompah its singing)
 streets filled with
 that quiet through the
 crowds it fills the crowds
it is the wonder
 my wonder of
 of southern
 Mexico
 this silence

here in Oaxaca my
Oaxaca the Oaxaca
I dreamed
constant fiestas
 50's Fellini parades
then these moments of devotion
 how it must have been
  when being human
meant being
 in wonder and awe

III. Casita Cannonball (San Pedro Ixtlahuaca)

Casita Cannonball

1.

we bought a
house a country cottage
and we named it
Casita Cannonball
for our loved
Cannonball
now gone

the old zen dog
old black Lab
would have liked it here
meditating on his paws
quiet
his unscripted life
his great great nephew
the chocolate Labrador
Apollo
who sometimes wanders
around the big house
we rent in Oaxaca Centro
the Primera Privada de Crespo
that was Cannonball's last
he'd
sun himself

in the front courtyard
on the back patio
a small happiness for us that
in his last year
his hips barely working
he didn't have to bear
a Brooklyn winter

Casita Cannonball
is in the *colonia* Rancho Buena Vista
Primera Privada de Libertad
the town San Pedro Ixtlahuaca

surrounded by mountains and farms and valley
there are three bulls
in the field next to us right now
later will come
goats and pigs, more bulls
two dogs

Apollo wonders at it all
he barks
and the two dogs bark back
at their new loud neighbor

roosters crow
tanagers in flight call
a thunderstorm is coming
it's all country noise
except for the silence
the Cannonball brings

he's everywhere here
so in his final home
he'll be

2.

the mountains sit
like clouds and the
clouds like clouds and
mountains

shadows of each other
and each other
shadowing and shining

together and
with the birds
the radio from
that old car
down the road
—*rancheras chilenas tango*—
they are
this morning

even for
our indoors
which looks out
with coffee and tea
and *mango papaya platano*
on the table

the gray

day was
only the gray of
the clouds of
clouded morning the
gray of small earthquakes
that one after another
shake the windows floor
we are supposed
to go outside or
stand someplace maybe
where the ground
won't open up
where you won't
fall in where the
world won't fall
on you or swallow

vivo bien

these dry season cicada
their song of desire
whistling/piercing

it's a month of long
love-making

an urgency
in trees

waving grasses

and those black and yellow birds fly

with cicadas in their beaks
sus picos

cicada season
scorpion season
cactus flower
to cactus fruit

and the sun
setting sun
the ghostly clouds
above
the mountains

we

open doors we
open windows we
find the day
breath
the morning the
air is full of
birdsong the air
filled with
birds

wandering empty midst

-mitten
durch uns
—Paul Celan

it's corn
and the roads spread
with the landscape's story
of what to why

between seen
and heard voices
approach:
it's a car on the road
tortillas empanadas
it's a truck
rolling by
with water or ice

omit skin

fugaz, fleeting
unless
the feeling
that strong
it can even defeat
time's relentlessness
tediousness

so out the door

beyond dirt road
where that
small river is dry
next month
with the rains
it will be flowing
will be more like what
we mean
saying *river*

by air sustained

by prayer by
river by
sleep by
night by
insect flight
bees and moths
yellow into the
sun the sun-
flowers and the
trees the river
it comes
always
back to the
river it's where
our water
comes from
it always
come back to the
air where

we who live
here are

los cambios

we call the casita
the country
as though it distills
into its small, unrolling green
every rural place
we've ever loved

and Centro, Oaxaca,
we call Brooklyn
because 3000 miles south, west
it contains in itself
a Brooklyn self, a Brooklyn soul

my mother said
you sound happy there
at the casita with
its mountains and valley
made of wood and adobe
and green cantera stone
my mother is old, she's sick
some days she forgets but her radar works

happy, she said
happy

how not

in the long unfolding suddenness
of where you ought to be

verisimilitude

sometimes only the truth
doesn't make
much sense

the whole day
the open screen door
moves soft
with the wind

so quiet it
might not even be
a door it could even be
a window

pleasing the gods

in this life
we never know

it's speculation:
charity, meditation, prayer

a poem, a meal
maybe a few hours

lost in the woods

maybe we are on a road

a highway
from one city to another

or from one city
to the mountains

or the same city
to the beach

the car takes the mountain turns
oxen eat straw

or corn or alfalfa
the water delivery guy calls out

agua, agua
and a sweet smell of burning wood

leaves a haze over the mountains
and the mountains now themselves

lost
from sight

every departure makes sense
cutting lavender

from the garden cutting
roses and rosemary

love and shadow

clueless mysteries
clueless songs
because old radio songs
come from the furniture *fabrica*
up the road
do I need a bed need some shelves
need a desk
do you need someone to hold
you all night
the song wants to know
do you want
a dove to come it should
fly out of the sky
the song wants
a kiss another kiss
but the *no y no*
no and no
answers to the
air

the water pump

not working probably
a short all the years
exposed to sun and rain
it costs 3000 pesos
for a new one
but a guy in town
will fix it for 600

his shop full of
pumps six guys
all fixing pumps
repairing rebuilding
in Spanish pump
is *bomba* which is also
a bomb or a fire station
and to pump *bombear*
no bombea
it won't pump which sounds
I think
a lot like *no bomb*

the old guy in charge
tells jokes he makes fun
of the other workers
one of them takes
our pump apart
a banging of hammer chisel
files screwdrivers wrenches
it's filthy rusted
they'll need to dry
the motor first
some black bugs jump
out of it the old guy jumps
matenlos matenlos
kill them he says kill them
no one laughs he's the boss
they're dead
he takes a breath another
looking at the pump he says

we'll have it ready
3 or 4 hours
he winks he wipes
his face with a hand
your wife will
take a
bath tonight

in between

what matters and no matter (*ni modo*)
the lines of sight and
the lines of hearing
because
no time to waste is
really more a way to say
how time can't be wasted
not when the morning cool
becomes afternoon rain
because that's the way
it is here
moment introduction to moment

what to do then
about the everywhere green?
the overgrown gardens?
or the unfinished pavilion
of wood concrete stone?

what to do
with lowing oxen?

with the slow moving
insects in the air
even in the afternoon rain?

something hot to drink? something cold?
some chocolate? some tortillas? some soup?
on pause
and expecting

call and song

the initial
give
overtaken by
the take
the please
so we know
what to do
with flowering trees
flowering cactus
with bushes of
Mexican sunflower

we turn to
the sun
a fine thing
for morning
we are
up and out
out of bed
down to the kitchen

there are flowers in the yard
the garden
the garden the house the land
the *colonia* the *pueblo*
the state the country the
world
it's all there
happening
we choose we who look and
get to go along

there is no

thing in life easy
now a *papamosca cardenalito*
vermillion flycatcher
in its own scarlet self
it guards the corn field
the golden haze
partly insect partly sun

then sleepy

we sleep
into sleeplessness
into our vital lives
our amazement at
precisely that
our amazement

we have

so many rooms
to enter leave
rooms
in which our dreams begin
with low voices or
we have birdsong and call
sounds of
church bells and fireworks
the beginning
of another fiesta
to mark another
time in the year
to remember
into memory
one saint or another
this time Saint Peter
patron saint of our *pueblo*
San Pedro Ixtlahuaca
last week it was a virgin
a little hilltop shrine
the week before a hero
it was the 19th it was the
20th century

later our neighbors work
their fields
corns beans squash
it's roosters hens
goats oxen a passing truck

love song

somewhere across
the shepherd's fields or
the farmer's fields or
the empty fields that
lead to the mountains
lead to the rivers

somewhere the way time
moves is time held
still patient impatient
with the universe it's
the way it happens the
way it happens

and to hold you to
have gone across this
airy room this room
to hold you to hold you
that's the story I
want to tell

careless

what new
words
collide
into beauty

being

the wild of
the wild
times and
the wild
of the
wilderness

in all this beauty
complete
beauty

it is no
strain
on the world
the sound
of hammer
spike
the oxen to
feed in the field

in another conversation

we dig in
the nest
the unwanted

dreams and
talk because
more about

money than

love we
dig

and we
hold to
the light

the many
flags
to which

we hold
no allegiance
we

here once
there were
other gods

here Sunday
children
run in that field

maiz
they run and watched by
strangers

definition

una tormenta here
in Mexico south

isn't a trial
isn't anger
or torture

it's a storm
and I'm in awe
the danger
and the beauty

it rolls and
roils in
over the mountain
it crosses the wide sky

in incendiary lightning
and sudden torrents
all darkness depth
all beauty
frightening beauty

where's your tempest now

that was
a storm not an
earthquake
though
the whole
sky shook
a force
forced onto
the land

around

we
we
we
just
couldn't
take
anymore
we
went
to sleep and slept
through
the thunder
and lightning

prediction

so many minds around
dawn will walk
lost into the valleys

and the streaked sky
with all the ribbons
will come closer

so the ribbons sunlight
will have names
that color the ways

we use our own:

we'll be the stars we'll
be the corn we'll be the

way growth is:
slow continuous rain and the
corn stretch toward the sun

not I

said the prince then all
the princesses and princes
went walking through time as
if time were the illusion
we once thought it was
but now know better and

they walk through time
princesses and princes
they walk through
alfalfa sunflowers
and the farmers and
the children of the farmers
stare at this unsurprised

because nothing new has happened
no mirage no illusion

breeze and trust

a quartet of flying insects
wouldn't mark the first time

for the dizziness of some affliction
for the spare teeth of
ripped and fading land
the voice sings
you always come back
but now it's too late
love is someplace else
flight consequence
a penny's worth
of thinking, of clandestine greetings

did you see
in the newspaper
endless photographs
we drink distilled water
or better wine
better tequila
or best mezcal
this far south
that's the prescription
like the deep red
into crimson
of the neighbor's bougainvillea tree
their goats never stop
with the bah bah bah
I imagine the life of the shepherd
noisy but maybe not
when the herds go down
as if in prayer
to eat
the shepherd sees

the thunder clouds, the lightning
feels the wind kick up
she heads the flock home
before this storm
invades the valley
their bah bah bah
all the way home

one call and another

a rooster
a goat
a blackbird
a dove
then the goat again
the goats again
then the birds
all birds
and that rooster leading
repeating repeating
the rooster insisting
repeat

then thinking

come with
the rain
no more
rain sun
rooster chorus
and hammered

wood
on Saturday
it's far off
music
another
version of
La llorona
from a field
beyond a field
each song and field

what's that

skittering on across
the roof
lizards maybe
not birds though
small white flocks
have been flying
through drying corn stalks
fading sunflowers
all morning

the roosters started
at four
the goats and sheep
screamed at six
as if the sun
needed greeting
they headed for
the river

the oxen
among themselves alone
feeding on dry grass
stayed behind

in the field

that white dog
has been slowly
walking sniffing pawing
hours

and for?

in the cool morning sun
in the coming rain

on the other
side of the fence
that large brown Apollo
barks because
emerging morning goats
complaining in their lines
they herd
they go they pass
Apollo barks and barks
all still ignored
by that small white
dog in the field

still unknown

beginnings marked by
a tanager, two tanagers
and something else
a fast flash of yellow
then small knives then
comes the falling into
this the dream
this dawn
then sleep sleep
and:

here's light here's blue here's day
and those mountains still dark and green
are not immortal either

the sun goes down

the beloved country
is somewhere else
maybe beyond the next mountain
the rain is at our backs
blue sky
in front
and with morning barking dogs
night barking dogs
we think of no future
save the present
its prospects
an example of

what a creative mind
might do with shadows
or prosperity or
perplexity
in over
our heads
we speak in tongues
become leaves and flowers
then palaces
then night
then flood
then night (again)
we sacrifice for
another kind of quiet
take the
remains
it's what we've earned
then only then
we ask forgiveness
having spent
love so poorly

ages of innocence

around our heads and
bodies like the bees
in that neighbor's house
who have turned
her hot water heater
into a hive when
you open the house front

door there are
black widow spider webs
black widow spiders
that's what we're used
to now
the bees their honey
the spiders

IV. Mi México

to understand the welcome

become the
stranger in
the room

the room
that lights
the house

that lights
the street
with white

and yellow
with something
like talk

something like
music a
wind a

voice a
heart a
sound a

welcome
welcome morning
welcome night we

say to each
other come
in come

over we'll
here
say enter

American charm

for Phil B. (Hip Hatchet)

there ought to be enough
a smile a wink a tip of the hat
some words that
reflect/respect/possess
grace

unless we live in
dangerous times
starting over times
unpredictable deaths and magic
we dress in black and white
we celebrate and mourn

elsewhere

it's all go to
be something big and
equal to the task of

randomness and
redemption
equal to
today
which is
sunny and blue
already loaded
with birds
in the air and trees
and across the street
yet again
a barking dog

destination

this isn't destiny the
way the word means though
destined might take us
all the way to the
mid-day meal
I think it
should be on the porch or
patio it's good to
eat outside we'll have
meat and tortillas someone
might have a mezcal or a
beer others lemonade
or water

can you believe
we live like this

is it what we were
coming to those years ago
in the plans though
not as I remember them

I remember sleepy towns
dusty towns as we
drank the beer the
mezcal I don't
remember thinking
this is where I'm going

you turn

your head and
look at me
I don't know
what you

see
on the other
side of
the world

it is dark
with here
the sun the
dawn

in love again

your hair falls
over your eyes
your face
we say
I was just thinking that
and
I was going to say
we admit the
borders for
years we've
been crossing we
still cross we
welcome

accident or chance

it was the evening's moment
a throw of the dice
the *comodín* the wild card
the joker the

stars in alignment for
a universal shift a
universal break and

we will be part of it we
the ones for the
universal trap the

universal question survival
our flashlights pointed to the
northern lights then the northern
sky up north the faraway snow

a return

which was it
being in Brooklyn
or in Oaxaca
which was
homecoming which
was home

lingo

someone asked
now that you live
in Mexico do you
ever write in Spanish?
a veces, supongo, sí

the workmen

clean the walls
scraping before painting
Jorge has found a
small laurel sapling
growing in a crack
which he plants in
the blue *maceta*

from which
he had just cleaned out
the small dead pine
the laurel he says
in five years you replant it
in twelve you'll have shade

it's in Atzompa

Roberto says
we can buy some
earthen iguana heads
he can put them on the roof
as rain gutters
out of terracotta mouths
rain waterfalls

year's end

here in Mexico south
from old clothes
old shirts and pants and shoes
dresses stockings
they make *monos por fin del año*
end of the year
life-size puppets
and at midnight burn them

goodbye old year
old sadnesses old demons
go bury the ashes

somewhere where
they'll fertilize
a garden or the land

hello new year
new morning sky
something better than
what's over
something dream and sun

with

this cool
morning breeze and
my eyes closed
all and all the sounds

one morning it was
a parrot singing talking
another morning a rooster who
crowed and crowed

who

you see on the street
ten cuidado
you might not
know the man playing
the harmonica the
accordion but
that little girl *there*

she holds
out a bowl she
asks for money she
already makes you
sad already for
her beauty

white gardenias

I bought
a few nights
ago on
the *zocalo*
a young woman
a gardenia
a rose in her
hair

now these
gardenias fill the
room a yellow
rose in the
center the
rose was
red in the woman's
black hair

this city is full

of trucks
of taxis bus exhaust

and in the morning
children sing in
the kindergarten
down the street
they sing and sing and sing
then they stop and
ringing church bells

the unbroken

is not the
undone not the
unstopped not
the moving fan
turning round
the room like a morning
wind the morning
wind is almost enough
it
fills the house
as it did
last year when we
came down
stairs opened the
doors the wind that
filled the house

that dog

only knows
to love

street dogs

but those
street dogs
they bare their teeth
they snap

but that dog
my dog
A-P-O-L-O
he knows
love I fear and
nothing but

Mi México

another night
of accordion and streets lights
guitar fireworks *(cohetes)*
they stream scream
vapor the air
that's filled with
the smell of corn
boiled grilled
the smokiness of
grilling meat
and the always chorus
buenas noches buenas noches
may your life go well
be blessed

la gente

se muere que muere
pero tu sigas siendo lo mismo

said an older man
to a friend even older
they were on line
at a food stand at
Llano Park

the people die they die
but you keep on the same

he might have said
the sky today or
those trees
all the unseen
changing writ in glass in
water clouds

keep walking

to the market to
the church the
café down the hill
stone streets the
bright sky blue almost
cloudless we've
entered the dry
season the nights get

cool even cold
clear the moon light last
night and I wore a
jacket walking Apollo

I slow

walk here noisy streets and
the quiet of this country
surrounds me the way it did
decades ago when I
first came here and
fell in love and thought
of the day for the rest
of my life I'd be here
and now it is
these streets in southern
Mexico the noise and
quiet me here

flight

you'd have to think
the air could hold
pieces of eight and
pieces of silver

or that the burden of
temptation was
the burden of mist in
the burden of trees

a rowboat
of decision across
the waters so slow
this morning
because in morning
lightning into music

the *tehuanas* have gone home
have left
their orange and black
flowers in the streets
an accordion plays
accordion songs
a street sweeper
leaves the flowers
he leaves
the boy his accordion
the little girl asking pesos
with her wooden bowl

he sweeps
the newspapers
headlines dust
he sweeps sometimes
the air

standards

we bear
loosely

the clothes we
wear the
loads we carry
of memory and
cloth as if
warp and woof are
the singular
practice of
our lives and

our lives move
as if what we
know what we
wait for or we
see as longing
is certain

like daily bread
like atoms and
electrons

or the
symphonic morning
of trucks and
birds of
wind in trees and
clouds and
lovers sleeping

you should have seen

how all the
young girls were
dancing in a
circle together they
were
holding hands they
were
flowers or autumn they
were dancing in they with
each other
there
was no music
we could
see only how
their skirts
moved their
arms moved
their
bodies
moved they
were in
their own
circle their
own world
their own
lives they
trapped
us they
enchanted

us we
who
disappeared
in the
end

leaf to leaf

over the years
things happen and
over this past year

we changed
a universe

we changed

we left Brooklyn
we arrived
Oaxaca and later then
San Pedro Ixtlahuaca

it isn't
the same sky
or sun

it isn't the
same language
every day
new words which is
new ideas which is

new meaning which is
new world which means
usually pleasantly
and not
unfamiliar

some mornings
the way the clouds
drift with the mountains
remembering six months
of dry season almost
no clouds at all
so the clouds
are part of the mountains
are as the mountains
and are of as sky is
sky

so the unfamiliar
becomes easier
normal
the unfamiliar is so
normal in a dream
so normal for
nothing to make sense
so in strangeness
you relax you sleep

V. Once upon a time

a history of poison

the house torn down

by so many enemies

so much staying power

so much surrender

all night we hear

the coming voices

incandescent evanescent immanent

whispers as if boats

the birds cried for hours

in the trees

except the *caracara*

that soars defiantly elegantly

comes on this way comes on the wind

above and below

another early promise

a history of rain

once upon a time

all the baby owls

were asleep

no one worked in the fields

it was quieter

a rooster some goats

Javier pounding

a fence post

into the ground

once upon a time

the llamas were asleep

llamas in pajamas

the books were closed

no more stories

throughout the skies

no one waited/everyone waited

buckets/water/water

for the gardens

a history of rivers

is

carried along far

farther

beyond

the horizons

from source to

destination

is love

then they break

and they bend

along

a history of wind

we rode the roads

the car top down

with funny rock and roll

for a dancing car

come on and play

you old so-so-so

you old happiness

come on and play

we're the never tired

boys and girls

a history of snow

once upon a time

a dream of barking dogs

Apollo barked

Cannonball barked

the living meet the dead

names silence

once upon a time

the porch doors

opened

filled the bedroom with light

snow was a memory

of cold far away

a name

About the Author

Mark Statman's most recent books of poetry are *That Train Again* (Lavender Ink, 2015), *A Map of the Winds* (Lavender Ink, 2013) and *Tourist at a Miracle* (Hanging Loose, 2010). His translations include *Never Made in America: Selected Poetry of Martín Barea Mattos* (Diálogos, 2017).*Black Tulips: The Selected Poems of José María Hinojosa* (University of New Orleans Press, 2012), the first English language translation of the significant poet of Spain's Generation of 1927, and, with Pablo Medina, a translation of Federico García Lorca's *Poet in New York* (Grove 2008). Statman's poetry, essays, and translations have appeared in fourteen anthologies, as well as such publications as *New American Writing, Tin House, Tupelo Quarterly, Hanging Loose, Ping Pong,* and *American Poetry Review*. A recipient of awards from the NEA and the National Writers Project, he is Emeritus Professor of Literary Studies at Eugene Lang College of Liberal Arts, The New School, and lives in San Pedro Ixtlahuaca and Oaxaca de Juárez, MX.

Lavender Ink

lavenderink.org